DISCOVERY READERS

# Where Are the Stars During the Day?

## A Book about Stars

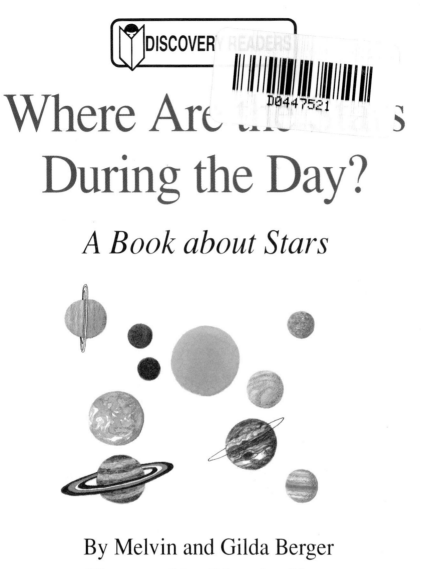

By Melvin and Gilda Berger
Illustrated by Blanche Sims

Ideals Children's Books • Nashville, Tennessee

The authors, artist, and publisher wish to thank the following for their invaluable advice and instruction for this book:

Jane Hyman, B.S., M. Ed. (Reading), M. Ed. (Special Needs), Ed. D. (candidate)

Rose Feinberg, B.S., M. Ed. (Elementary Education), Ed. D. (Reading and Language Arts)

R.L. 2.0 Spache

Text copyright © 1993 by Melvin and Gilda Berger
Illustrations copyright © 1993 by Blanche Sims

Published by Ideals Publishing Corporation
Nashville, Tennessee 37214

Printed and bound in the United States of America.

**Library of Congress Cataloging-in-Publication Data**

Berger, Melvin.
   Where are the stars during the day?: a book about stars/by Melvin and Gilda Berger; illustrated by Blanche Sims.
      p.   cm.—(Discovery readers)
   Summary: Basic information on our solar system, its components, their movements, and their likely history.
   ISBN 0-8249-8644-X (lib. bdg.)—ISBN 0-8249-8607-5 (pbk.)
   1. Astronomy—Juvenile literature. [1. Astronomy. 2. Solar system.]
I. Berger, Gilda. II. Sims, Blanche, ill. III. Title. IV. Series.
QB46.B49   1993
523.8—dc20                                             92-18200
                                                          CIP
                                                          AC

*Discovery Readers* is a registered trademark of Ideals Publishing Corporation.

Produced by Barish International, New York.

Look up at the sky on a clear night.
You see lots and lots of stars.
They look like little points of light.

Look up at the sky during the day.
You don't see the stars at all.
Where are all the stars?

The stars are still in the sky.
You just cannot see them.
The sun is so bright that it blots out the
little points of light.

4

Looking at the stars is the same as
    watching a movie.
You can see them best in the dark.
Imagine that you're watching a movie.
It is dark in the movie theater.

Then someone opens a door.
A bright light floods the screen.
It blots out the light of the movie.
The movie fades on the screen.

Someone shuts the door.
Now it is dark again.
You can see the movie.

The dark theater is like the night sky.
The light from the door is like the sun.
When the door is open, you can't see
the movie.
When the sun is out, you can't see the
stars.

Why does the sun only shine during the
day?
Why does it *not* shine at night?

We all live on Earth.
Earth is always spinning.
You can't feel it turning around.
Yet it makes one complete turn every
twenty-four hours.

Your house is someplace on Earth.
Part of the time, your house faces the
    sun.
It is daytime.
The sun's bright light shines in the sky.
You can't see any stars.

At other times, your house faces away
 from the sun.
Outside it is dark.
The sun does not shine in the sky.
You *can* see the stars.

Think of Earth as a spinning toy top.
Make believe you're standing on the
top.

As the top turns, you face different
　　ways.
First you face a bright light.
Then you face away from the light.
Round and round you go.

The bright light is like the sun.
When you face it, the stars disappear.
When you face away, the stars appear.

Did you know that the sun is also a star?

The sun looks much bigger than all the
other stars.
Yet the sun is not the biggest star.

The sun seems to give off much more
light than all the other stars.
Yet the sun is not the brightest star.

Why does the sun look bigger and
    brighter than any other star?
Because it is much, much closer to
    Earth.

The stars' lights are like the lights on a
    car.
Far away they look like little points of
    light.
Close up they look bigger and brighter.

The sun is about ninety-three million
     miles away from Earth.
That seems like a great distance.
But it is not far for a star.

The next nearest star to Earth is called
   Alpha Centauri.
Alpha Centauri is much, much farther
   from Earth.
The distance is twenty-five trillion
   miles.

Imagine that you have magic boots.
Each giant step you take is ninety-three
   million miles long.
One giant step takes you to the sun.

You must take almost 300 giant steps
   to reach Alpha Centauri!
The rest of the stars are even farther
   out in space.

19

The sun and the other stars are alike in
     two main ways.
They give off light.
They give off heat.
Stars are made of hot, swirling gases.
Most of the gas is hydrogen
     (HIGH-droh-jen).

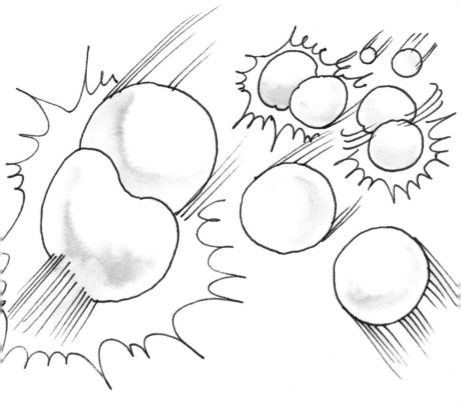

Hydrogen gas is made up of tiny bits
   called atoms.
The hydrogen atoms jump this way and
   that.
They keep bumping into each other.
Sometimes they bump so hard that they
   stick together.
Then there is a flash of light.
There is a burst of heat.

Every second, billions of hydrogen
   atoms join up.
Billions of light flashes go out into
   space.
Billions of bursts of heat go out into
   space.

The bursts make great streams of light and heat.

The streams of light and heat never stop flowing.

The sun is so close that you can see its light.

You also can feel its heat.

Other stars give off as much light and
heat as the sun.
But they are much farther away.
You can hardly see their light.
And you cannot feel their heat at all.

Starlight travels a long way before it
reaches Earth.
The light shines from the star.
It passes through trillions of miles of
space.

Then it goes through the layers of air
around Earth.
Finally you see it.

The layers of air are always moving.
They bend and break the starlight.
The light shimmers and shakes.
The stars seem to twinkle.

Would you like to see your toes
   "twinkle" like the stars?
Try this the next time you take a bath
   or go swimming.
Look at your feet through the layers of
   water.
As the water moves, your toes seem to
   change shape.

The water is like the layers of air.
It moves and scatters the light.
Your toes are like the stars.
They seem to "twinkle" in the moving
water.

People have been looking up at the
stars for ages.
Long ago they noticed something
strange.
Most stars seemed to stay in the same
place.
A few seemed to keep moving.

Ancient people called the moving
objects planets.
The word means "wanderers."

Today we know of nine planets.
They travel around the sun.
Earth is one of the planets.

 Mercury: closest planet to the sun

Venus: hottest planet

Earth: home planet

Mars: red planet

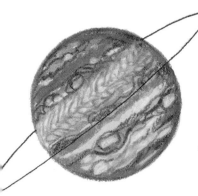

Jupiter: largest planet

Saturn: planet with broad, bright rings

Uranus: planet with narrow, dark rings

Neptune: dark and icy planet

Pluto: most distant planet

31

Some stars form groups in the sky.
The most famous group is the Big
    Dipper.
It looks like a cup with a long handle.

Seven bright stars make up the Big
    Dipper.
Three stars are nearly in a row.
Connect them with an imaginary line.
That's the handle.

The handle lines up with another star.
This star and three others form a shape.
Connect these stars with imaginary
    lines.
That's the cup.

You can find the Big Dipper every
    night of the year.
It is always in the northern sky.
Yet it doesn't always appear in the
    exact same place.

Winter
    —in the north
    —low in the sky
    —handle points down

Spring
    —toward the east
    —high in the sky
    —handle points to the side

Summer

    —toward the west

    —high in the sky

    —handle points up

Fall

    —in the north again

    —low in the sky

    —handle points to the side

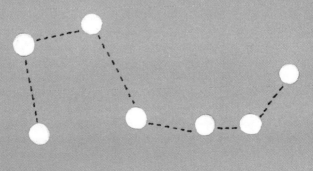

Two stars make up the front of the
    dipper.
Those two stars point up to a bright
    star.
The bright star is called the North Star.

Sailors know that the North Star is
   always in the north.
They can use it to tell direction.
They can steer their ships by the North
   Star.

The winter sky has another well-known
group of stars.
These stars seem to outline a human
figure.
It looks like a powerful man holding a
giant club.

Someone thought the figure looked like
Orion (oh-RYE-un).
Orion is the great hunter of Greek
legend.

Some groups of stars that form pictures
are called constellations.
Orion is a constellation.
It has more bright stars than any other
constellation.

39

Here is how to find Orion.

Face southeast on a dark, winter
evening.

Look halfway between the horizon and
straight up.

Do you see three bright stars in a row?

They make up Orion's belt.

Their names are Alnitak, Alnilam, and
Mintaka.

The stars leading down from his belt
represent a sword.

The brightest star in Orion is
at the tip of his right foot.

This star's name is Rigel (RYE-jell).

The star representing his other foot is
called Saiph (SAFE).

In summer and fall, you can see
    another group of stars.
They make a white path across the sky.
We call this white path of stars the
    Milky Way.

The white path looks different through
  a telescope.
The telescope lets you see many
  separate stars.

The Milky Way contains about 100
    billion stars.
Such a huge family of stars makes up a
    galaxy.
A galaxy contains gas, dust, and
    planets, as well as stars.

Our sun is one of the stars in the Milky
    Way galaxy.
All the other stars you can see are in
    the same galaxy.

The Milky Way galaxy looks like a
    giant pinwheel in space.
Most of the stars are in the middle.
The rest are in arms curving out from
    the center.
Our sun is in one of these arms.

The whole Milky Way galaxy spins
around in space.
It turns like a pinwheel in the wind.
As it spins, the sun and Earth turn too.

Our Milky Way galaxy is one of many
galaxies in space.
Scientists think there may be 600
billion galaxies in all.
Together they make up the universe.

Look up at the sky the next clear night.
Find some stars and planets that you
   know.
Look for the Milky Way.

Picture the other giant galaxies out in
  space.
Enjoy the stunning sight!

# *Index*